Chile

Energy, Environment and the

Mapuche

By

Paul F. Davis

- Contents -

Introduction   5

Energy Security   9

Geothermal   17

Coal Industry   19

Air Quality and Public Health   23

Air Pollution and Environmental Decontamination   24

Electric Cars   27

Environmental Victories   29

Punta Arenas Gas Strikes   31

Agricultural Reforms and Food Security   35

Mapuche – People of the Earth   36

Human Rights   55

Culture and Values Shape Institutions   59

Environmental Threats Along the Border   60

Environmental and Economic Cooperation   67

Importing Energy   71

Lessons from the Mapuche   73

Bibliography   77

Introduction

The foundation of all environmental issues is land. Land disputes are a reoccurring theme with the Mapuche, who seemingly have never been fully compensated, nor restored by the Chilean government for the lands that were stolen from them. If the Chilean government cannot honor land and property rights of its indigenous people, can it be expected to preserve the environment and equitably use its energy?

Ongoing water scarcity across Chile has complicated the nation's energy scenario causing President Sebastián Piñera and Energy Minister Laurence Golborne to carefully examine and evaluate the way forward, as they seek to creatively engineer solutions and access alternative energy sources.

The Chilean government is forecasting the possibility of a dry year in 2011 without its main source of energy, hydroelectric plants, being used to maximum capacity due to lack of rainfall. 'Water-generated energy' once 'accounted for 70 percent of total production' in Chile back in 2002. Hydropower has since declined significantly over the past decade and 'is predicted to account for just 41 percent' of Chile's energy needs in 2011 (Briggs and Gallegos).

Perhaps the Piñera cabinet should employ some of China's technology to manipulate the skies and generate rain. China spends $100 million a year and employs 50,000 people for rainmaking to increase its annual 'rainfall by 210 billion cubic meters' for the needs 'of 400 million people' (Wade).

These options aside, Golborne is trying to avoid winter energy rationing in Chile and is considering measures to promote an energy saving initiative 'used by past governments in Chile' to encourage the people (not the copper industry which uses a third of all energy annually) 'to use energy sparingly' (Briggs and Gallegos).

Many say the lack of rainfall has been caused by La Nina, the strongest weather cycle in 35 years which has led to reductions in rainfall up to 46% in some regions of Chile (Bernama).

The 'president of the National Agriculture Society,' suggests Chile 'consider building more water reservoirs and dams' (Bernama).

The Santiago Times reported the La Paloma reservoir in the Coquimbo Region, has reserves 74% below its capacity. "The drought caught us with already very low reservoir reserves, so the effect has been more pronounced," said Fernando Santibanez, professor of climatology at Universidad de Chile (Bernama).

As fossil fuels fill the gap for hydroelectricity declines due to water shortages, contamination levels and

CO_2 emissions will increase in Chilean cities. No long-term policy commitments were made by Golborne, who is taking 'this year to define new environmentally friendly and sustainable energy standards' (Briggs and Gallegos).

'Liquids remain the world's largest energy source... given their importance in the transportation and industrial end-use sectors,' which is 'expected to grow from 86.1 million barrels per day in 2007 to 92.1 million barrels per day in 2020, 103.9 million barrels per day in 2030, and 110.6 million barrels per day in 2035' (U.S. EIA).

The good news is by relying on 'different energy sources' over the next 10 years, Minister Golborne noted Chile can be expected to double its energy production capacity (Briggs and Gallegos). Unfortunately for now however, due to the drought in Chile, the 'main energy distribution system (SIC),' which 'contributes 60 percent of Chile's total energy generation and serves 93 percent of the population,' will consist primarily of 'fossil fuels' (Briggs and Gallegos).

Dry weather could potentially reduce 'hydroelectricity's share of overall production' in Chile to 41 percent, which in turn would lead to an increase in the contribution of fossil fuel, the latter of which is predicted to 'provide 58 percent of production to SIC' (Briggs and Gallegos) under such conditions. That translates into increased carbon emissions, which remain an ongoing concern in Chile, a nation ranked 51st in the world and 6th in Latin America (Briggs and Gallegos).

Energy Security

An energy blackout left half of Chile without power on February 3, 2011 for up to an hour. *The Canadian Press* (CP) reported, 'The failure in a substation brought down the electricity grid in nine of Chile's 15 states.'

The reduced hydroelectric capacity across Chile as a result of an ongoing drought 'has emptied reservoirs and forced Chileans to use more diesel and coal for fuel, which makes energy more expensive and increases the carbon dioxide emissions that cause global warming' (CP). My watery eyes in Santiago confirmed air pollution is a problem. Therefore 'expanding clean energy sources is a top priority' for Chile (CP).

Chile's energy security has been bolstered by international agreements with Argentina, Colombia, and Peru, but could be further improved were it to negotiate an agreement with bordering Bolivia. Potential nuclear energy agreements, coupled with the prospect of future collaboration and cooperation between Chile and the United States are also promising as President Obama prepares to travel to Chile in March 2010.

Interestingly, the Chilean mining industry is apparently 'unharmed' by Chile's national energy contingency plans (Gardner and Soto). Perhaps because the consumption and conservation effort is primarily expected to encourage decreased usage among the Chilean people, not the mining industry that consumes a third of all Chile's energy.

President Piñera however reminded 'all Chileans' of 'the late 90's... severe power cuts, which meant very significant costs for Chilean families and their quality of life, and also the productive apparatus' of the country (Briggs). The presidential decree sought to act early and avoid possible power cuts in the future.

Rationing in the north, where Chile's heavy industry is located, is among the suggested ideas to help protect energy supplies in the south. Chile's north consumes 60 percent of the total energy produced in the country. Yet the top producer of copper in the world hopes to 'avoid the specter of energy rationing' (Gardner and Soto), lest its voltages be lowered and the quality of its copper be damaged during the production process.

'Big mines usually keep contingency generators to keep the voltage steady… and also have dedicated power lines directly from the central power grid' (Gardner and Soto), but as 'rain shortages force generators to rely on costly fuel-driven plants' the cost of copper production rises along with its price in international markets.

Although President Sebastian Pinera is telling Chileans to 'reduce energy use by 5 percent to avoid shortages' and advising the 'public to be sparing with energy consumption… to avoid power cuts in the future' (Gardner and Soto) no such restrictions or advisories have been issued to the copper industry thus far.

With water reserves at a ten-year low, one measure mentioned by Golborne to reduce energy consumption includes "reducing voltages by between 5 and 10 percent" (Gardner and Soto). The larger concern is "saving water in reservoirs to be able to use it towards mid-year when water shortages can be even more pronounced," Golborne said.

Perhaps the water shortage will finally force Chile to look beyond hydroelectric power to meet its energy needs. Certainly investing more heavily in renewable energy and pursuing negotiations with bordering Bolivia and Peru to supply Chile with energy are other viable options.

Despite possible energy shortages and blackouts, analysts remain confident given thermoelectric plants remain available as a backup option (Gardner and Soto). Apparently 'energy-hungry miners reaping a copper windfall' are not scathed by the drying up of Chile's hydroelectric power thanks to renewable energy as a backup option (Haynes). Meanwhile elsewhere in Chile 'electricity costs' are expected to go 'soaring' and make 'renewable power sources like wind, solar and geothermal more attractive' (Haynes).

Although investment in renewable energy will benefit Chile over the long-term, until renewables are adequately developed and available, 'generators must rely on plants powered by costly imported oil and gas' (Haynes), potentially leading to inflation.

Since 'Chile's energy prices have nearly tripled in five years' (Haynes), renewable energy such as wind, solar and geothermal power offer attractive alternatives for long-term stability. Record high copper prices should enable the mining sector to invest in renewable energy technology to reduce their cost of production and move Chile in the right direction for sustainable energy. Among the progressive mining companies heavily investing in renewable energy, 'state miner Codelco has committed $700 million to a 250 MW wind farm that may be the largest in Latin America when finished, and world No. 3 copper mine Collahuasi is exploring geothermal energy to tap Chile's immense volcanic activity' (Haynes).

"With copper at $4 per pound, you can pay what you want," said Francisco Aguirre, executive director of Santiago engineering firm Electroconsultores (Haynes), speaking on the mining industry's move to develop renewable energy sources.

Among the new developments is 'Chile's second-largest wind farm, the 48 MW Monte Redondo complex 200 miles (325 km) north of Santiago. Energy and Mining Minister Laurence Golborne said wind power remains a promising resource given Chile's extensive wind-swept coastline' (Haynes).

Ongoing earthquakes heighten Chile's energy concerns and need to develop renewable sources. The Chilean people are familiar with energy blackouts from the days following last year's massive earthquake, which left transmission lines and energy infrastructure damaged. 'Chile's central grid supplies more than 90 percent of the population and is most likely to be hit by the energy squeeze because of its reliance on hydro power. The far northern grid, which powers miners in the copper-rich Atacama desert, relies on thermoelectric plants fired by coal, gas and diesel' (Haynes).

Chile's energy regulations require 'that generators incorporate non-conventional renewable energies in their output' (Haynes), which began at 5 percent last year and are expected to reach 10 percent by 2024. A very ambitious measure requiring 20 percent usage of 'alternative energy by 2020' (Haynes) was even discussed by Chile's 'previous energy minister,' which Golborne himself aspires to achieve. "Today there is no country in the world with 20 percent of its power produced by renewable energy. However that is the long-term aspiration of our country," Golborne said (Haynes).

As for the methodology of computing the contribution of renewable energy to the total energy consumption and usage, 'Chile's alternative energy law counts output from hydroelectric plants smaller than 40 MW along with sources like wind power, which has grown to around 170 MW capacity in Chile since the first turbines were installed in 2008' (Haynes). Conversely most other countries that even come close to a 20 percent ratio cheat a bit by also counting 'coal, fossil fuels and nuclear energy' (Haynes).

Geothermal

'Although no geothermal power plants are currently producing geothermal energy on the continent, several

South American countries - led by Chile and Argentina - are working to encourage geothermal development through implementing policy measures that incentivize the development of all renewable energy resources, including geothermal. Chilean local and international mining companies are now looking to develop geothermal resources to help meet the electricity needs of their operations. The government has already sold a number of geothermal exploration and development concessions to local and foreign geothermal developers in order to address issues stemming from increased energy consumption and demand. ...In the next 10-15 years as more and more countries seek to ensure energy security, as well as to reduce their carbon intensity, geothermal power generation' (Power) will be a viable option for many South American countries.

Coal Industry

The Chile's capital goods corporation (CBC) recently reported, 'Nearly half of Chile's planned investment in energy production over the next four years will use coal as its primary fuel' (Briggs). Since coal is the most economically cost effective (though arguably the most environmentally harmful) means of producing energy, many favor its 'continued use as essential to meeting Chile's growing energy needs over the coming years' (Briggs). The high levels of 'carbon output' heavily contribute to 'contaminating green house gases' that thwart public health and cause environmentalists to consistently oppose 'the creation of new coal-burning power plants around the world' (Briggs). Chile however is planning to invest further in coal in 5 of 13 'regions: Atacama, Bio-Bío, Valparaíso, Maule, and Antofagasta' (Briggs). 'The CBC estimates 90 percent of new energy generation between now and 2014 will be generated from 23 power stations and 53 hydroelectric dams' (Briggs).

Energy generation is expected to 'account for 39 percent of the investments registered with the CBC through September 2010, making it the sector with highest level of investment in Chile,' over the next 4 years and is predicted to overtake the mining industry, 'which accounts for… 30 percent of investments' (Briggs).

Chileans across the country have risen up to oppose Alerta Isla Riesco—a coal plant project underway. Words are insufficient and a poor comparison to this gut wrenching video that visually captures the magnitude of what excessive coal use will do to the Chilean environment. A must see video concerning the dangers of the coal industry in Chile can be found at <http://www.youtube.com/watch?v=KI2xDPKtYQg>.

'The incomplete combustion of fossil fuels,' coal being one of the most heavily polluting, 'releases black carbon into the air' to 'increase global warming, being second only to CO_2' (Wikipedia). The soot produced 'will absorb solar energy and transport it to other areas' such as the Beagle Channel 'where glacial melting occurs. It can also darken Arctic ice reducing reflectivity and increasing absorption of solar radiation' (Wikipedia). This explains why when I was on a cruise recently traveling through the Chilean fjords, the tour guide said the Chilean glaciers have been increasingly melting over the years.

'Segio del Campo, former general director of the Guacolda coal-burning generator owned by AES Gener, has been appointed Chile's new undersecretary for energy. According to the *Santiago Times*, the new undersecretary held executive positions in energy companies in both the Dominican Republic and in Argentina before taking his position at Guacolda in 2002' (Anderson).

'With his boss Laurence Golborne now busy overseeing both the mining and energy ministries, del Campo is expected to be given great latitude in developing the nation's energy policy, notwithstanding criticism that he will be creating policies that directly impact his former (and future?) employer Guacolda' (Anderson).

To get a glimpse into Chile's energy future, del Campo as head of Guacolda 'was among the first to strongly criticize proposed new emissions standards for coal-burning generators' (Anderson). Although Chile has massive 'renewable energy potential showcased by its sun-drenched deserts and it windy coastline, Chile is projected to have 28 coal-burning electricity generators up and running in 2011, accounting for roughly 60 percent of the nation's energy supply' (Anderson).

Chile's appointment of a former energy executive who is content to burn coal across the country, reminds me of former U.S. President Bush's 'Texas chainsaw administration' handing over '100 top environmental posts to representatives of polluting industries' causing 'a devastating rollback of three decades of progress' (Kennedy).

Air Quality and Public Health

The World Development Indicators (WDI) on air quality show: "Where coal is the primary fuel for power plants, steel mills, industrial boilers, and domestic heating, the result is usually high levels of urban air pollution—especially particulates and sometimes sulfur dioxide—and, if the sulfur content of the coal is high, widespread acid deposition' (2007 WDI).

'The Metropolitan Region of Santiago has been declared as nonattainment area for carbon monoxide (CO) according to the Environmental Monitoring Assessment completed in 2010' (Sanhueza). 'Air pollution continues to pose a significant threat to health worldwide' (WHO Air Quality) and to Santiago in particular' (WHO Air Quality).

Air Pollution and Environmental Decontamination

'The regional Special Commission for Decontamination of Chile's capital, Santiago, was formed in 1990. The issue of regulating passenger car emissions was one of the first initiatives on the commission's agenda... (Bauner and Laestadius 157).' In Sept. 1992 'a decree required every new car in the capital regions to be equipped with a catalytic converter' (157). Instrumental factors contributing to the success of the measure were: 'the effective and efficient adoption and adaptation of foreign technology, policy, and market space, Chile's common understanding of the need to reduce emissions, and prevalent strong economic growth permitting widespread car ownership and renewal' (Bauner and Laestadius 157).

Yet 'the primary driver for introduction of unleaded fuels in Chile' was 'not the toxic effects of lead to human health' (Bauner and Laestadius 179), which provides enlightenment concerning the chronology and motivation historically behind the 'interaction of regulation and innovation' (158).

Some principles by which regulation makes innovation more friendly (159-160):

- Focus on outcomes, not on technologies

- Enact strict rather than lax regulation

- Regulate as close to the end user as practical, while encouraging upstream solutions

- Employ phase-in periods

- Use market incentives

- Harmonize or converge regulations in associated fields

- Develop regulations in synchronization with other countries or slightly ahead of them

- Make the regulatory process more stable and predictable

- Require industry participation in setting standards from the beginning

- Develop strong technical capabilities among regulators

- Minimize the time and resources consumed in the regulatory process itself (159-160)

What occurred in Chile involved 'elements of innovation, and cooperation as well as competition between different car manufacturers' (162).

Economic growth and development in Chile is based on 'the export sector,' 'exploitation of natural resources,' and 'foreign investment rather than on organic growth of national firms and competence' (165).

Electric Cars

Electric cars have been discussed for use in Santiago for short commutes to lower emissions and reduce air pollution. Reva, an Indian manufacturer, offers a very reasonably priced electric car for around $3,000. Some advantages of electric cars (Boxwell 9-11):

- An electric car moves smoothly and quickly.

- The lack of gearbox makes for easy driving with a smooth power delivery.

- Electric motors are exceptionally quiet with no vibration.

- In heavy stop-start traffic, electric cars are easier to drive.

- At lower speeds, electric cars feel more responsive.

- No fuel needs to be purchased at an annoying filling station.

- Range is rarely an issue since most people don't drive more than 50 miles (80km) from their homes and those who do travel longer do so only a few times a year.

Governmental legislation, economic incentives, tax breaks and other creative mechanisms all can encourage the use of subways, electric cars, and car pooling for those who use conventional vehicles. Combining innovation and legislation that incentivizes conservation of fuel and the environment, will sufficiently motivate Chileans to do the right thing both for their pocketbooks and the planet in which we live.

Encouraging automobile drivers to transition over time to using electric cars (while not threatening the lifestyles of those who already own conventional cars) such as REVA from India that are economical and environmentally friendly, would be a complementary policy to pursue along with furthering the extension and construction of subway rail lines throughout Santiago.

Environmental Victories

Health, environmental concerns, and lobbying pressures have delayed the proposed '2,750 MW Patagonian dam project HidroAysen and the 2,350 MW coal-fired Castilla plant proposed by Brazil's MPX Energia' (Haynes), a project which would alter and severely affect the region's ecosystem.

GDF Suez was another company that had to back off a planned 540 MW power plant in August 2010, after President Pinera at the urging of activist environmental groups compelled GD Suez to relocate its 540 MW power plant amid public protests that the plant would 'harm an endangered penguin reserve' (Haynes).

A third victory for environmentalists was the delay of two 340 MW coal plants, projects that were postponed following last year's catastrophic earthquake. A fourth triumph for environmentalists concerned whalers from Japan, who had come to Chilean waters to poach whales in Chile's Antarctic waters. Whaler Nisshin Maru suspended their whale hunt when the environmental group Sea Shepherd's 'aggressive' sabotage tactics of 'tying ropes in the Nisshin Maru's propellers, hurling corrosive acid at the ship, and provoking collisions' (Seitz) complicated their operation. Sea Shepherd's efforts gave the Japanese whale killers (20,000 a year) a taste of what it feels like to be hunted.

Punta Arenas Gas Strikes

Recent gas strikes in southern Chile, derailed thousands of tourists (including a friend of mine) who had their vacation plans altered so they could experience Chilean politics and protestation. Nation unions' "sympathy strikes" attracted little empathy from Chile's Interior Minister Rodrigo Hinzpeter, who didn't hesitate to 'invoke the State Security Law to assure public order' (The Clinic).

An interview with Punta Arenas Mayor Vladimiro Mimica (who supported the strike) provides insight into the public outcry concerning the government's natural gas price increase.

Mayor Mimica said of President Pinera and his administration in power, "The President has been in

Magallanes and he has only met with to or three of his aides. In his last trip here, I was only able to talk to him in the street" (The Clinic).

The fact the Mayor of Punta Arenas cannot get a private meeting to speak directly with the President, tells me Pinera is avoiding him. This appears to be a reoccurring theme in Chilean politics. Southern Chile, unless useful for generating energy or some resource for economic exploitation (such as salmon, seafood, and lumber), tends to be forgotten and marginalized as if it were its own separate country. Yet whenever protestation against the government in Santiago occurs, suddenly the military and police are called upon to quiet the uproar in the south to keep the country in tact and society in "order."

Mayor Mimica said: "The strike began …because the government was unwilling to find a political solution (to the gas price hike). …you just can't continue playing with your calculator, crunching figures, and giving Chileans misinformation. When the government speaks so glibly that our gas prices are six times lower than what is paid elsewhere in the country, they need to add a fact or two. ...The gas consumed in most of Chile is not from Magallanes, but is imported from Asia, Malaysia, Trinidad and Tobago. This is very high priced gas and has no relationship at all to the gas that is consumed in Punta Arenas. ...The gas that we pay for in Magallanes is 600 percent higher than what is paid in Argentina's Patagonia, where the climate is the same. The government isn't telling the truth. ...The government is giving priority to the money paid to Metanex to export gas..." (The Clinic). State and foreign industry profitability (the latter of which can often pay off politicians to cooperate) seems to be the prevailing pattern.

Mayor: "There is no regionalization policy. We here in Magallanes have supported all the subsidies given to the

Transantiago transit system in the capital city, just like other regions. So where is the government's regionalization plan? And now they are about to privatize the waste water systems throughout the country. Where is this money going to end up once the systems are sold? In Santiago! …We want an end to the secret way gas policy is done in Chile. How was the gas price negotiated between ENAP and Gasco? Why is there a confidentiality clause in that contract when we have a transparency law? When everyone in Chile has the right to know how deals like that are negotiated? How are gas prices set? How and why are sale prices set for Metanex? And for the people living in our communities? We want the secrecy to end. …It looks to me like the gas we have here in Magallanes is only for export. …The state's most important role is to look after its citizens. …But …this government …is safeguarding the interests of private investors" (The Clinic).

Agricultural Reforms and Food Security

Chilean policies and practices toward the Mapuche jeopardize human, environmental, and national security.

During the 1973 coup against Popular Unity socialism, 'the military dismantled an ambitious agrarian reform program ...expropriating nearly half of Chile's agricultural land' and redistributed it 'mostly to male heads of household' (Tinsman). No doubt the militarized government saw the 'massive rural labor movement' numbering 'a quarter million peasants, 95 percent of whom were men' by 1973 as a potential threat that must be squashed (Tinsman).

The focus instead was to 'develop free markets and integrate Chile into the world economy,' having the abrupt affect of reversing previous agrarian reforms. 'By the mid-1980s, women comprised almost half of the fruit industry's estimated 300,000 temporary workers. ...Labor conditions were intensely exploitative, while the climate of fear and restrictive labor laws made overt challenges to the system impossible' (Tinsman 12-13). The fruit industry essentially emasculated male laborers, removing their access to steady work, and stripped them of the land parcels received under agrarian reform.

Mapuche – People of the Earth

The Mapuche identity is specific to their relationship to the ecosystems they inhabit. In the indigenous language "che" means people, whereas "mapu" represents the earth or world (Mallon 261). Hence combining the two we get "the people of the earth," making the Mapuche most vital to Chile's current environmental and energy struggles.

Another subgroup of the Mapuche are the "Lafken" – meaning the people of the water. They who live off the aquatic resources (fishing, shellfish, and the seaweed they collect) are also an important part of Chile's environment and economy (Mallon 261).

Modern day capitalism often disrupts the environment, pollutes the air we breathe, contaminates the water we drink, fragments society, and disrupts public health.

The few who dare to live in simplicity are often ridiculed, despised, and ostracized by the "civilized" (who have been capitalized upon) in the heavily populated and polluted cities. The Mapuche who live off the land, through their values and customs, can help the government and people of Chile to rediscover life balance, personal harmony, and again appropriately value the priceless beauty of the earth.

Until the people of Chile can return to the land and its cultural heritage, they will forever be duped by foreign corporations from afar who come only to rape its resources and pillage its people. Empty political promises made by presidents who have come and gone, have yet to fully indemnify the Mapuche for generations of injustice, thievery, and underhanded dealings. "The lack on constitutional recognition for indigenous peoples, the lack of approval of ILO Convention 169 on Indigenous Peoples and… lands bought with money from the Land and Water Fund" not "considered indigenous lands unless they were already considered such before the purchase" (Mallon 290) are just a few of the injustices that have frustrated the Mapuche.

Debates over the fine print in Chile is nothing new. The 2009 presidential campaign promised to give mothers a six-month maternity leave, has since been manipulated and arguably reduced based on the fine print of the legislation (Gallegos).

Unfulfilled promises, misperceptions, and final revisions via cleverly written legislation appears to be the legacy of Chilean politics. Tell the people what they want to hear to get elected, after which politicians do as they please when drafting the fine print.

Land is the foundation and essence of all environmental issues. Chilean land occupations and takeovers is the history of the Mapuche people. Chilean leaders historically favored "the division and privatization of Mapuche land-grant communities... to keep the Mapuche separate from Chilean society and economy" (Mallon 3-4).

National development in Chile has a historical precedent of being favored over the rights of the Mapuche. The Agreement of Nueva Imperial did not result in 'new treatment of indigenous peoples in Chile' (Richards 132), as the Chilean state repeatedly preferred national development over human rights.

'The construction of the Ralco hydroelectric plant… along the Bio-Bio river in Pehuenche territory' (132) involved simultaneous destruction of Mapuche 'sacred cemetaries and other religious sites' (132), flooding ancestral lands, and relocating Pehuenche families. Although the dam was widely opposed from the beginning by the Mapuche on the grounds of its disruption of cultural, environmental, and economic foundations of community life, these concerns were rejected and disregarded.

A second example and 'demoralizing symbol of the privileged position of national development above Mapuche rights' (134) is the Chilean forestry industry (Richards 134). Beyond disrupting the natural ecosystem, the Chilean forest industry has impoverished the Mapuche substituting native forests 'with quick growing pine and eucalyptus' (134-135) which strip the soil of necessary nutrients and water needed for farming and raising animals. Hence Chilean authorized industry and energy producing developments have thwarted the environment and livelihood of Mapuche communities.

To further add salt to the wounds of the Mapuche, the Arauko Malleko Coordinating Network illegally occupied plantations, cut and burned trees down on Mapuche lands, blocked roads, and sabotaged equipment (135).

State exploitation of the environment and Mapuche people 'as of 1996, the state had granted 1,357 concessions for mining exploration or exploitation in ancestral Mapuche territory, 104 of these being 'actually in Mapuche land. Seventy-five percent of water rights in the same territory had been granted by 1996,' while 'only 2 percent of these were granted to Mapuche individuals' (135).

The guarantees of 'water and subsoil rights for indigenous communities' were provisions Congress conveniently removed 'from the final law' to expedite development favoring the 'forestry and tourism industries' (135).

Is it any wonder therefore why today 'Mapuche feel deceived by the Chilean state' and 'CONADI, which was supposed to have been an instance of co-governance between the state and indigenous peoples' (135). Instead CONADI has turned out to be a cleverly manufactured device used by the state to provide the appearance of a protection mechanism to give voice to the indigenous peoples, when in reality to the contrary at times CONADI has been used as a 'tool of the state' (135).

In addition, the state has manufactured "national security threats" in which "the rule of law" allows them to clamp down on Mapuche peaceful protestors thwarting development and with whom the state disagrees. Countless Mapuche have been jailed and made to be 'political prisoners' (135). Environmentally disruptive developments with the aid of the state bulldoze over the Mapuche and ecosystem simultaneously, causing region IX to be 'the most heavily militarized' zone in Chile, as 'police repress' peaceful protestors with 'tear gas and billy clubs' (135).

Theft, redistribution, and exploitation of Mapuche lands historically in Chile have been responded to by favoring a 'paradigm of national identity and development' to strengthen the state's economic position (Richards 149).

Despite Manuel Manquilef, the first Mapuche congressman, being elected in 1925, the bill he introduced to divide indigenous lands (Mallon 4) did not necessarily serve the Mapuche well. The Chilean government determined to keep the Mapuche from progressing, cleverly made it mandatory for the Mapuche to confirm the original boundaries of the land and provide the original land title as issued by the Chilean government prior to any division of lands taking place (Mallon 4).

At "the end of the 19th century," when the Chilean army defeated the Mapuche and the "state handed over reduced quantities of land to Mapuche communities between the Bio-Bio and Tolten rivers" such land grants were registered and received legal title. Presumably these "documents gave legal protection to the indigenous individuals originally settling there and to their direct descendants... In practice however local state institutions tended first of all to protect the rights of non-Mapuche property owners, and little was done to preserve the interests of indigenous communities" (Mallon 6).

Land usurpations peaked between 1900 and 1930, "after a community received its 'original title' "...national and foreign colonists" (6) illegally seized their lands. At best

Mapuche land restitution has "occurred in only 16% of the cases, with an additional 12% in which partial restitution is achieved (28% in all)" (Mallon 288).

Former President Patricio Aylwin proposed "an Indigenous Law" (inspired by the 1978-90 indigenous movement) "to repay part of the 'social debt' the state owed…the indigenous peoples of the country" (186). Despite the gross human injustices committed and dire need for moral reconstruction to restore order to civil society, the law that was finally passed in 1993 was trimmed down and a gutted version of the original first conceived (186-187) leaving the landless Mapuche disappointed and frustrated.

Thereafter the Mapuche were slowed down in their progress for land reparations and restitution by legal verbiage, structural difficulties, applications, and stipulations such as 'subsidies', 'agricultural credits', and 'inheritance or kinship rights' causing more tensions and resentment (187-

190). The criteria by which communities could apply to legitimate a land subsidy application to achieve state recognition and gain a right to restitution, wearied and frustrated Mapuche resuscitating "old fears and misgivings" (190-191).

Further cumbersome was Chile's "changing definition of community," which suddenly constituted "ten adults belonging to the same indigenous ethnic group" (Mallon 192). The broad manner in which "indigenous" could be defined opened a loophole for others beyond the Mapuche to happily apply for new land also.

Such have been the challenges of the Mapuche and the cleverly created contradictions and complications of the Chilean government's politicians to delay full restitution.

Where the Chilean government has failed, the Church must lead the way by example and make restitution to the

Mapuche people and communities whom they have wronged (Mallon 12).

A historical look at Chile's treatment of the Mapuche examined the *El Mercurio*, a right wing newspaper that represents the conservatives in Chile. An unbiased British academic reported the newspaper generally portrayed the Mapuche in images as terrorists. The newspaper's attitude toward the Mapuche mentioned was:

"Their attitude is, the ninth and tenth regions are areas of insecurity, this is really awful, because we want foreign companies to invest, and we need to bring down the law on these Mapuche radical terrorists" (Attwooll). Yet the Mapuche are simply fighting for their soil being drained by forestry companies, the environment dam projects like Ralco are destroying, and land being stolen from their communities.

The extent of a nation's human and property rights are good indicators of civil society (or the lack thereof) and thus the future state of the economy.

Education and cross-cultural sensitivity training from the inner circles of government to the elementary classrooms is undoubtedly needed in Chile. Although more Mapuche teachers are active in Chile's educational system and bilingual intercultural education is being introduced in some areas where there is a high percentage of Mapuche, the historical revisions and cultural nuances removed from textbooks are important.

Mapuche political representation is virtually scarce and sadly lacking, which not only affects indigenous peoples but their lands and environment as a whole. The Mapuche are a buffer between the Chilean government and the environment providing a powerful voice of environmental consciousness and accountability.

Chile's former President Salvador Allende admitted, "There are Mapuches whose land was stolen many years ago and who are living off half a hectare... People think of them as an alien race; they are physically and morally degraded" (Foulkes).

In regard to moral degradation, it is useful to study the Mapuche religious history and practice of witchcraft and homosexuality (Bacigalupo), to see how Spanish missionaries and Europeans coming into Chile could so easily stereotype, ostracize, and alienate them (and by doing so pass on generationally a similar attitude and disposition to Chileans). The unique spirituality of the Mapuche may in part explain (although not justify), why Chileans have found it easier to demonize and dehumanize them as a people.

To this day old mindsets looking down upon the Mapuche and using them as scapegoats to distract attention from real issues continues to be a problem in Chile.

Psychologically and subconsciously Chile's governmental leaders and military quite possibly have been given to this tendency of labeling Mapuche as troublemakers rather than citizens worthy of equal rights. One example is former President Bachelet's request made to the U.S. government and FBI to look for possible connections between Chilean indigenous groups and terrorists abroad (Silveira).

The Bachelet administration's inquiry focused on the indigenous conflicts in Chile's Araucanía Region, which the *Santiago Times* (*ST*) says "have historically been greeted with over-dramatized responses from local politicians and sensationalized" by "selective coverage by local media outlets" (Silveira).

Nothing credible, nor evidentiary has come forth whatsoever thus far to incriminate any Mapuche activists and peaceful protestors. Ironically, "the 2009 cables analyzing the Mapuche conflict in Chile underline 20 years of failed policies and insufficient legislation from Concertación governments, bureaucratic barriers to recovering ancestral land, and widespread poverty and discrimination that fuel anger and frustration in the long-marginalized communities" (Silveira).

The priest's words in the movie *Machuca* come to mind: "Respect each other no matter who you are or where you were born."

Although Pinochet is long gone, the U.S. recognized his era's antiterrorism law continues to be applied "to enforce harsher sentences on indigenous activists, supported by... politicians such as Sebastian Piñera, who is now in office" (Silveira).

'In a batch of cables from the U.S. Embassy in Santiago,' it was stated, "The Mapuche have sought greater autonomy in recent years over what are claimed as ancestral lands in the Araucania region, about 400 miles south of the capital... The indigenous group, Chile's largest, remains mostly marginalized in the broader society" (Hernandez).

The U.S. Embassy in Santiago criticized the Bachelet administration for being "slow to focus on indigenous issues" (Hernandez). Mapuche leader Aucan Huilcaman said the Bachelet government "never wanted to solve the Mapuche problem" (Hernandez).

Mapuche nonviolent protestation is far more the norm in the region than violent outbreaks. President Allende said, "We don't think that the problems facing Mapuches can be solved simply with agricultural reforms. This is a problem of cultural anthropology, of race. We have sent them doctors, pediatricians, anthropologists and sociologists as well as the Agricultural Minister" (Foulkes).

Mapuche respond differently to 'modernization, capitalism, and foreign influence' (317). Mapuche spirituality challenges sociopolitical hierarchies and dominant Chilean gender norms, resulting in stereotypes of sexual "deviants" being put upon the Mapuche.

Society and governments however can tend to stereotype and make snap judgments pertaining to a people group that can be debilitating and perpetuate past pains for generations, while holding many in a cycle of defeat wherein they spiral repeatedly through difficulties some of which originate from being socioeconomically disenfranchised altogether.

We therefore must endeavor to know people not by their momentary behavior, but by the person within and potentially who they can become if given the proper opportunity and capable mentoring.

Hence President Allende recognized "it is not a short-term problem," but "something that will be with us for years. In the eyes of the law, the Mapuche are considered children without rights, so the situation is not going to change overnight. We need a lot of time to erase the memory of what has been done to them over the past century and more" (Foulkes).

Yet to erase such bad memories and break the cycles of defeat causing so much pain for the Mapuche and the nation of Chile, conciliation must precede reconciliation. Past efforts to reconcile with the Mapuche have proven ineffective due to a historical ongoing lack of goodwill and friendly relations. Hence to reverse the curse and animosity of the past, the Chilean government must acknowledge human rights violations committed against the Mapuche people and make full restitution for lands stolen, economic opportunities lost, and suffering caused. Only after national repentance, constitutional legal reform (forbidding partisan retractions at a later date as presidential administrations change), and reparations are paid can reconciliation draw near.

Many Mapuche have shown themselves able to adapt and to ensure their voices are heard through online blogging and citizen media platforms such as Twitter to highlight widespread devastation, governmental neglect, and abuses in rural areas. The Feb. 27, 2010 earthquake exposed social problems usually hidden behind a facade of stability (Vinas).

Human Rights

Impartiality and independence seems to be greatly lacking in the Chilean courts according to a 2011 Human Rights Watch (HRW) World Report which 'criticized the excessive and inapplicable use of military tribunals in cases involving civilians. The police and military's poor handling of ongoing indigenous Mapuche group's protests, particularly those in Chile's southern Araucanía Region, is a major focus of the report' (Briggs). The police consistently get lenient sentences for their human rights abuses, while sustaining "law and order" for the common good.

In Sepember, 2008 'Chile's Supreme Court reduced the sentences of retired Army Col. Hugo Guerra Jorquera and civilian Luis García, two participants in the murder of 15 farm workers in Liquiñe (Region XIV) in the weeks following Chile's September 11, 1973 military coup' (Snyder). Pinochet's 'team of military and civilian gunmen set on strengthening the dictatorship by eliminating any remnants of Chile's reformist movements' carried out the murders 'on October 10, 1973' (Snyder).

Fear still exists today among rural workers due to the systematic killing of farm workers by the military carried with the aid of less than civil landowners.

'Germán Rodríguez, a leader of El Surco, one of Chile's best known rural confederations, said that rural fear marks most campesino communities to this day' (Snyder).

Rodriguez mentioned talking about unions today is still very difficult due to the grip fear has on many.

Unions have been reduced from representing 40% of Chilean workers as in 1973 to today representing only about 13% (Reichard 78) due to the use of force, fear, and fragmentation of opposition communities. Hence democracy exists only in appearance, as military repression has contained activism, grassroots movements, and disconnected the indigenous people and many farmers in rural areas.

'El Surco officials challenge official government figures of 324 campesino murders, saying the figure could actually be as high as 3,000' (Snyder). With about 8% of Chilean campesinos being organized in cooperatives or associations, the lax rulings the Supreme Court hands out to murderers serving state interests is alarming and sends a clear message that reformist movements and farm workers' protests will continue to be controlled and labeled "terrorists" whenever they aroused opposition to whatever government is in power in Santiago.

'According to Amnesty International and the UN Human Rights Council, 250,000 Chileans had been detained for political reasons by the end of 1973. Summary executions, disappearances and killings in staged armed confrontations became a norm' (Snyder).

The way the Chilean justice system is currently set up, 'uniformed police fall under the jurisdiction of the armed forces' and are tried by 'the military appeals court, which is composed of three military judges accompanied by two civilian appeal judges' (Briggs).

By containing rural reform movements and the Mapuche, the Chilean government simultaneously has effectively silenced the largest populist base of opposition to land acquisition, division, exploitation, and environmental disruption. They who live on and from the land are ideally the most galvanizing force and people group able to address Chilean environmental concerns. Hence by forcibly controlling and "legally" containing them, Chile has open access to re-alter much of the nation's land and environment according to its will—which usually is pro-industry and haphazard development throwing environmental concerns and consequences aside.

Culture and Values Shape Institutions

'History shapes the culture and values, which give rise to society's institutions. ...Social values permeate a society and all of its institutions. Such values are responsible for the forms that these institutions take' (Reichard 80).

Chile's history of human rights abuses and neglect of the indigenous peoples, along with the use of force against peaceful protestors reveal that development often trumps everything. This means the environment is often forgotten along the way too as the people most closely connected to the land who can protest are quickly contained.

Historically, Chile's seizure of nitrate rich lands from Brazil 'had a profound impact on the economic development of the nation' and inherent social values. The tendency therefore was to 'reinforce the export orientation of the Chilean economy, which made it largely subservient to foreign interests' (Reichard 82).

Environmental Threats Along the Border

'An Argentine federal judge suspended the application of six articles of the country's new glacier protection law' (Henao) in November, 2010 to permit Barrick Gold Corp. to proceed with its controversial Pascua Lama project.

Reuters reported Barrick is building a large mine, which many fear lies under a glacier. 'The glacier protection law bans mining and oil drilling on glaciers and the areas surrounding them' (Henao). Argentina gives provincial governments the right 'to decide how to manage their natural resources" (Henao) even if that means disrupting and destroying them apparently. Rather than halting the mining company from potentially disrupting the environment and requesting an environmental impact assessment be performed before making a ruling, 'the judge suspended the article' (Henao).

The Argentine government therefore presently seems committed to economic development more than preserving its environment. That being said, Chileans should beware of the potential environmental hazards and risks of sharing a border with Argentina given these new policy developments.

The *Financial Times* reports 'Bolivia's plans for the next five years are ambitious' and 'no less than an industrial revolution' (Schipani). Bolivia's energy minister said, "We want to industrialize Bolivia and leave behind the model of pure extraction and export of natural resources by gaining aggregated value. And we want this to be done through the energy sector with the exploitation and commercialization of the energy resources and with new policies to accelerate exploration" (Schipani).

As Bolivia shifts to 'more added value production, starting with gas derivatives such as fertilizers' (Schipani) the potential environmental hazards and unwanted spillover across the border into Chile should be monitored.

The *New York Times* reports, 'The reorganization of South America's energy relationships is being closely followed by countries trying to limit their reliance on energy-rich nations that are in political flux or that use their resources as a political lever....' (Romero and Schipani).

"The new projects in South America offer a striking example of how countries can cut their umbilical dependence on pipelines," said Carlos Alberto López, a former Bolivian energy secretary (Romero and Schipani).

Chile is a potential market for Bolivian gas through 'ship-borne imports, in which the fuel is cooled into liquefied natural gas for transport from exporting countries and reheated on delivery. This increasingly common transport method has provided substantial competition with pipelines in some markets' (Romero and Schipani).

'Bolivia itself once had plans to export liquefied gas by sending it first to a Chilean port, from where it would be shipped north to Mexico or the United States. But the plan caused so much outrage — driven in part by historical tensions with Chile and by resentment of the political elite here who had championed the project — that it was a major factor in an uprising by Bolivia's indigenous population in 2003' (Romero and Schipani).

'Cracks are already emerging in Bolivia's energy industry as the focus of international energy companies in South America shifts decidedly to Brazil, which is developing its own new discoveries of offshore oil and gas, and away from Bolivia and Venezuela. Prices for Bolivia's gas fell sharply in 2009, with income from gas exports declining 39 percent to $2.1 billion, according to the Bolivian Hydrocarbons Chamber' (Romero and Schipani).

"As foreign companies slow investments here, drilling for new fields is almost at a standstill," Bolivian energy consultants said (Romero and Schipani). What this means for Chile is Bolivia is an attractive alternative to supply its gas needs and given the sad state of affairs in the Bolivian energy sector negotiating a reasonably low purchase price for Bolivia's gas should be fairly easy to accomplish for Chile. The primary impediment is Bolivian aspirations to regain a coastline that belongs to Chile, which along with a nationalization of the energy industry politically serves to regionally alienate potential purchasers of Bolivia's gas and thereby further "box itself in" (Romero and Schipani).

Nothing attests more to poor geopolitics than Bolivia's inability to sell its natural gas reserves to neighboring Chile. Although Bolivia 'has the second-largest natural gas reserves in South America after Venezuela" (Garcia), it has failed to capitalize on the nearby Chilean market.

Perhaps Bolivia could learn a bit about the gains to be had by resolving territorial disputes along the border by studying Chilean and Argentine relations.

'Aylwin also negotiated agreements with Peru to end a dispute that, like the conflicts with Argentina, had simmered for more than a hundred years since the War of the Pacific. Lowering tensions facilitated economic agreements that, in turn, opened new markets for trade and investment, ensured critical supplies of Argentine oil and gas, and helped to break Chile's diplomatic isolation' (Parish 163-164).

'Joint projects integrated electrical grids across the border, to supply Chile with Argentine oil and gas via transandean pipelines, and to give each country access to the other's Atlantic and Pacific ports' through "bioceanic corridors" resulted in 'formed partnerships and produced mutual benefits that finally began to create a constituency in each country for cooperation. Entrepreneurs quickly followed the political opening with expanded trade and cross-border investments, and private sector initiatives became a central component of the growing interdependence' (165).

Environmental and Economic Cooperation

The historical struggle between Argentina and Chile for Patagonia provides many lessons for Chilean international and domestic environmental, energy, and economic policy. The International Expert Workshop (IEW) on the Analysis of the Economic and Public Health Impacts of Air Pollution recommends improving communications, extending collaboration, providing 'guidance and support for researchers, advances in methods, and resource support for data collection, assessment, and research' (1163).

'The statue of the Christ of the Andes commemorates the termination of a sixty-year boundary controversy that on several occasions brought Argentina and Chile to the brink of war' (Perry 347). Nineteenth-century Chile astutely acknowledged the importance of 'the mineral wealth of the Atacama in the north and the Straits of Magellan in the south' (Perry 363). Modern day Chile understands geography, but politically have seemingly severed good relations with the south preferring rather to merely exploit and lord themselves over the region. Such a position and posture in Santiago toward the south is sure to eventually incite revolt (and beyond that of the past). The elite in government in Santiago should therefore beware and deal prudently with humility toward its brothers in the south lest they become bitter enemies and grow increasingly hostile

The lessons Chile can learn from Brazil and Paraguay is cooperation saves time, blood, and national treasure the latter of which can be more wisely invested and utilized to benefit countries on both sides of the border through joint collaborative efforts, ventures, and initiatives. These benefits come in many forms such as improved transnational relations, tourism, security, economic advancement, environmental preservation, and national stability (a prerequisite for foreign direct investment).

Brazil in 1957 felt the Guaira Falls belonged to them and sought to harness its hydroelectric power, by launching an offensive militarily effort to control the La Plata Basin. Five years of disputation and disagreement with Paraguay over the basin and falls led to a peaceful negotiation of 'the terms of the Itaipu dam' and 'an end to the border dispute' (Wolf and Newton). 'Cooperation between Brazil and Paraguay had ripple effects into areas of conservation and preservation. When the environmental concerns around the construction of the Itaipu basin came to the forefront, the two countries implemented two joint projects, the Gralha Azul and the Mymba Kuera, to minimize the effects of reservoir flooding on the regions ecology, deforestation in the region and moved the wildlife most affected by the dam to biological reserves' (Wolf and Newton).

'The Intergovernmental Coordinating Committee functions' along the La Plata River basin provide Chile some ideas and historical precedent from which to draw when moving forward with its energy policy and evaluating potential joint ventures with its neighbors (Wolf and Newton).

'Today there are 130 dams along the River, two of which are widely known, the Itaipu and the Yacureta. Itaipu is the largest hydroelectric project in the world and a result of a 1973 bilateral agreement between Paraguay and Brazil. The generating capacity is 26,000mW and supplies 26% of all of the electricity for Brazil and 78% for Paraguay with zero emissions' (Wolf and Newton). A previous source of transnational controversy, the Itaipu dam is now a symbol of 'cooperation over a shared water resource' (Wolf and Newton).

'The ALMA project is a partnership between Europe, Japan and North America in cooperation with the Republic of Chile' (Alma 1) to erect a 'single research instrument composed of up to 80 high-precision antennas, located on the Chajnantor plain of the Chilean Andes in the District of San Pedro de Atacama, 5000 m above sea level. ALMA will enable transformational research into the physics of the cold Universe. Providing 'astronomers a new window on celestial origins, ALMA will probe the first stars and galaxies, and directly image the formation of planets' providing 'astronomers unprecedented sensitivity and resolution' (3).

Importing Energy

Peruvian President Alan García's government plans to produce nearly eight times the power the country currently has 'by harnessing the country's Amazonian rivers' and increasing use of the nation's 'plentiful supplies of natural gas, and wind and solar power' (The Economist). The disruption of ecosystems and displacement of 10,000 people doesn't deter Peru, which plans to become 'a regional energy hub, exporting electricity to Brazil and Chile' are said to have begun to 'be put into effect' despite protestation from green groups (The Economist). The Marañón river, also known as Peru's "energy artery" has 'the capacity to generate 10,000MW from six dams.' , Peru's 'energy ministry proposes to grant a concession to build a 1,500MW fossil-fuel power station near the border' to 'use natural gas from Peru's big Camisea field' (The Economist) to be transported via pipeline to the Chilean border.

China's railways are currently being linked throughout East Asian countries to be greatly used to transport oil and gas to the chief financier of the operation.

South American integration linking Peru and Chile's electricity grids in like fashion is a wise move for the energy sectors and economies of the region. Damming rivers, disrupting ecosystems, and displacing thousands of residents however are inexcusable and likely to come with innumerable long-term consequences and social costs. As for Chile, their mines in the northern desert will be more than happy to use Peruvian electricity.

Lessons from the Mapuche

The Mapuche are spiritual and in touch with the natural. The Mapuche see the Catholics and Christians throughout Chile as a conflicted people. The latter say they celebrate the God of the resurrection, yet their images and religious artifacts primarily personify a crucified Christ. Unlike 'these ignorant wigkas (non-Mapuches),' Mapuche believe in a God who is good and helpful, while giving them 'strength and courage' (Reuque 104) to overcome societal injustice and peacefully coexist with the earth which God created.

Though 'the wigkas say we're all brothers' (Reuque 104) their governmental policies and practices show otherwise repeatedly giving the Mapuche 'the short end of the stick' (105), while dehumanizing and marginalizing them in society and stealing and destroying their lands environmentally. The Mapuche struggle therefore has teeth and provides to the Chilean people needful perspective about the contradictions and unjust 'internal workings' of the national political system, which prioritizes party interests over people (216-217).

As for the Mapuche, brotherhood is a concept their communities have cherished and practiced for a very long time. At the outset of the Mapuche movement, their name change to "Ad-Mapu" meant "with the land," or "part of the land"; it being 'a guiding principle of life for the

Mapuche people" that both unifies and establishes balance 'between humans and nature' (118).

That 'balance and reciprocity' (118) is what the environment in Chile is repeatedly crying out for. Could it be the very earthquakes below shaking the nation of Chile are a sign and symbol testifying against the ongoing natural violations and indigenous community disruptions occurring daily from the decisions being made at the highest chambers of Chilean government?

The future hope or fatal destruction of Chile is found in its relationship to its indigenous people and their ties to the land. 'Even though non-indigenous peoples have cut down the forests and destroyed nature, they haven't been able to completely destroy indigenous peoples or Mother Earth' (Reuque 209).

When a nation, its government, and people lose its connection to the natural world and begin to accept the theft of land, forcible relocation of communities, pollution of rivers, erosion and depletion of soil, exploitation of trees, birds, animals, and mineral wealth without fully considering the environmental consequences and properly taking the time to first formulate policy and plans to achieve sustainable and peaceful development, the backlash from the earth and its people most closely tied thereto is inevitable.

Bibliography

2007 World Development Indicators. World Bank. Web. 19 Feb. 2011. <http://siteresources.worldbank.org/DATASTATISTICS/R esources/table3_13.pdf>.

"ALMA Exploring the Universe at Millimetre Wavelengths ALMA Brochure Explore 2007." *ALMA Brochure Explore 2007*. ALMA at ESO, July 2007. Web. 19 Feb. 2011. <http://www.almaobservatory.org/images/pdfs/alma_broch ure_explore_2007.pdf>.

Anderson, Steve. *"Former Coal Executive To Manage Chile's Energy Policy In Wake Of Ministerial Shake-Up"* – *Santiago Times*, 7 Feb. 2011.

Attwooll, Jolyon and Administrator. "National Identity And The Mapuche in Chile" – *Santiago Times*, Sept.17, 2003.

Bacigalupo, Ana Mariella. "The Creation of a Mapuche Sorcerer: Sexual Ambivalence, the Commodification of Knowledge, and the Coveting of Wealth," *Journal of Anthropological Research*, Vol. 61, No. 3 (Autumn, 2005), pp. 317-336. University of New Mexico. Web. 2 Feb. 2011.

Bauner, David and Laestadius, Staffan. "The Introduction of the Automotive Catalytic Converter in ChileAuthor(s): David Bauner and Staffan Laestadius." *Journal of Transport Economics and Policy* 37.2 (May 2003): 157-99. Print.
Published by: University of Bath and The London School of Economics and Political Science.

"BERNAMA - Insufficent Rainfall - Chile Prepares For Energy Rationing." Malaysian National News Agency :: BERNAMA. 11 Feb. 2011. Web. 19 Feb. 2011. <http://www.bernama.com/bernama/v5/newsindex.php?id=563072>.

Boxwell, Michael. *Owning an Electric Car 2010 Edition.* Warwickshire UK: Greenstream, 2010. Print.

Briggs, Mark. "Chile's Energy Investments Strongly Favor Coal Power." *Santiago Times*, 20 Jan. 2011. Web. 19 Feb. 2011. <http://santiagotimes.cl/business/other/20550-chiles-energy-investments-strongly-favor-coal-power>.

Briggs, Mark. "Chilean Government Decrees Energy Rationing Powers." *Santiago Times*, 10 Feb. 2011. Web. 19 Feb. 2011. <http://www.santiagotimes.cl/news/other/20732-chilean-government-decrees-energy-rationing-powers>.

Briggs, Mark and Gallegos, Ignacio. "Chile Discusses Immediate Energy Options For 2011." *Santiago Times*, 4 Feb. 2011.

Briggs, Mark. "Human Rights Watch Condemns Chile's Institutional Obstacles To Human Rights." *Santiago Times*, 4 Feb. 2011. Web. 19 Feb. 2011. <http://santiagotimes.cl/news/human-rights/20676-human-rights-watch-condemns-chiles-institutional-obstacles-to-human-rights->.

"Close to the Sky | Biological Heritage in Alma Area." *ALMA Observatory Book 2007* - ESO in Chile, 2007. Web. 19 Feb. 2011.

<http://www.almaobservatory.org/images/pdfs/alma_obser
vatory_book.pdf>.

Foulkes, Rob and Administrator. "Interview With Former
President Salvador Allende." *Santiago Times*, Sept.29, 2005.

Gallegos, Ignacio. "Chile's Magallanes May Rise Up
Again: Coal Mine Project Upsets Environmentalists."
Santiago Times, Feb.1, 2011. Web. 19 Feb. 2011.
<http://santiagotimes.cl/news/environmental/20643-chiles-
magallanes-may-rise-up-again-coal-mine-project-upsets-
environmentalists->.

Gallegos, Ignacio. *"Proposed Maternity Leave Extension
Draws Controversy In Chile." Santiago Times*, Jan.25, 2011.
Garcia, Eduardo. "Morales Shakes up Cabinet at Start of
Second Term." *Reuters*. 23 Jan. 2010. Web. 19 Feb. 2011.
<http://www.reuters.com/article/2010/01/23/bolivia-
energy-idUSN2312748420100123>.

Gardner, Simon and Soto, Alonso. "Mining Giant Chile
Moves to Head off Energy Squeeze | Reuters." *Business &
Financial News, Breaking US & International News |
Reuters.com*. 09 Feb. 2011. Web. 19 Feb. 2011.
<http://www.reuters.com/article/2011/02/10/chile-energy-
squeeze-idUSN0922615520110210>.

"Global Dimming." *Wikipedia, the Free Encyclopedia*. 12
Jan. 2011. Web. 19 Feb. 2011.
<http://en.wikipedia.org/wiki/Global_dimming>.

Haynes, Brad. "UPDATE 1-ANALYSIS-Costly Chile
Power May Jolt Renewable Energy | Metals & Mining |
Reuters." Reuters.com. 10 Feb. 2011. Web. 19 Feb. 2011.
<http://af.reuters.com/article/metalsNews/idAFN10276093
20110210>.

Henao, Luis Andres. "Argentine Judge Grants Glacier Law Exemptions for Pascua Lama." 2 Nov. 2010. Web. 19 Feb. 2011.
<http://www.mineweb.com/mineweb/view/mineweb/en/page34?oid=114>.

Hernandez, Daniel. "Chile sought U.S. help over 'radicalized' Mapuche Indians" – Los Angeles Times, Dec. 15, 2010, Web. Feb. 2, 2011.
<http://latimesblogs.latimes.com/laplaza/2010/12/chile-wikileaks-mapuche-bachelet.html>.

"Hydro-powered dreams: Hopes and Fears of a Regional Energy Hub. " The Economist. 10 Feb. 2011. Web. 19 Feb. 2011.

"International Expert Workshop on the Analysis of the Economic and Public Health Impacts of Air Pollution: Workshop Summary." *NCBA - National Center for Biotechnology Information*. Environmental Health Perspectives, Vol. 10, Number 11. Nov. 2002. Web. 19 Feb. 2011.
<http://www.ncbi.nlm.nih.gov/pmc/articles/PMC1241074/pdf/ehp0110-001163.pdf>.

Kennedy Jr., Robert. "Texas Chainsaw Management." *Vanity Fair*. Conde Nast Digital, May 2007. Web. 19 Feb. 2011.
<http://www.vanityfair.com/politics/features/2007/05/revolvingdoor200705>.

Langewiesche, William. "Eden: A Gated Community." The Atlantic Monthly - June (1990). Print. Four sections.

Machuca, a film by Andres Wood, explores Chile's bloody 1973 coup through the eyes of two 12-year-old boys from opposite extremes of society.

Mallon, Florencia. *Courage Tastes of Blood: The Mapuche Community of Nicolas Ailio and the Chilean State, 1906-2001*. 2005, Duke University Press. Print. 261.

Mountford, Charlotte. "Pregnant Woman In Chile Denied Abortion Of Fetus With No Brain." *Santiago Times*, Jan.28, 2011.

Parish, Randall R. "Democrats, Dictators, and Cooperation: The Transformation of Argentine-Chilean Relations." *Latin American Politics & Society* 48.1 (2006): 143-74. Print.

Perry, Richard O. "Argentina and Chile: The Struggle for Patagonia 1843-1881." Academy of American Franciscan History Jan. 36.3 (1980): 347-63. Print. Source: The Americas. Published by: Academy of American Franciscan History.

"Power Engineering International." *Global Geothermal Power* Nov. 18.10 (2010): 50-53. Print.

"Ralco Hydroelectric Plant." *Wikipedia, the Free Encyclopedia*. 18 Oct. 2010. Web. 19 Feb. 2011. <http://en.wikipedia.org/wiki/Ralco_Hydroelectric_Plant>.

Reichard, Stephen. "Ideology Drives Health Care Reforms in Chile." *Journal of Public Health Policy* 17.1 (1996): 83-98. Print.

Reuque, Paillalef Rosa Isolde, and Florencia E. Mallon. *When a Flower Is Reborn: the Life and times of a Mapuche Feminist*. Durham, N.C.: Duke UP, 2002. Print.

Richards, Patricia. Pobladoras, Indigenas, and the State: Conflicts over Women's Rights in Chile. New Brunswick, NJ: Rutgers UP, 2004. Print.

Riesco, Alerta Isla. *Alerta Isla Riesco*. Rec. 14 Jan. 2011. Web. 19 Feb. 2011. <http://www.youtube.com/watch?v=KI2xDPKtYQg>.

Romero, Simon, and Andres Schipani. "Neighbors Challenge Energy Aims in Bolivia." *New York Times* 9 Jan. 2010. Print.

Sanhueza, Pedro, Jaime Pizarro, Claudio Vargas, Monica Torreblanca, and Manuel Passalacqua. "Health Risk Estimation Due to Carbon Monoxide Pollution at Different Spatial Levels in Santiago, Chile." *Environmental Monitoring and Assessment* 167.1-4 (Aug 2010): 165. Print.

Schipani, Andres. "Bolivia Launches Ambitious Energy Plans." 26 Aug. 2010. Web. 19 Feb. 2011. <http://www.ft.com/cms/s/0/fc451fa2-b11e-11df-bce8-00144feabdc0.html#axzz1Dr5b9rJi>.

Seitz, Jackie. "Japan Cuts Short Whaling Season In Chilean Antarctica." *The Santiago Times*. 17 Feb. 2011. Web. 19 Feb. 2011. <http://www.santiagotimes.cl/news/environmental/20792-japan-cuts-short>.

Silveira, Alison. "Wikileaks: U.S. Looked Past Chile's Sensationalist Media Bias In Mapuche Coverage" – *Santiago Times*, Dec. 15, 2010.

Snyder, Jason. " Chilean Courts Reduce Prison Sentences for Human Rights Abusers." *The Santiago Times*. 28 Sept. 2008. Print.

The Canadian Press. *Chile considers energy rationing after blackout brings down half the nation*. 3 Feb. 2011.

The Clinic. "What's Going On In Chile's Southern City of Punta Arenas?" – *Santiago Times*, Jan.18, 2011.

The Holy Bible: New King James Version. Thomas Nelson, 2010. Print. 1 Samuel, Proverbs, Romans, Hebrews, Haggai.

Tinsman, Heidi. "Politics of Gender and Consumption in Authoritarian Chile, 1973-1990: Women Agricultural Workers in the Fruit-Export Industry." Latin American Research Review 41.3 (2006): 7-31. Print. Published by: The Latin American Studies Association.

"U.S. Energy Information Administration / International Energy Outlook 2010." *EIA Highlights*. Web. 19 Feb. 2011. <http://www.eia.doe.gov/oiaf/ieo/pdf/highlights.pdf>.

Vinas, Silvia. *Chile's indigenous Mapuche speak out online* – BBC. 11 March 2010. Web. 5 Feb. 2011.
  < http://news.bbc.co.uk/2/hi/8560995.stm>.

Wade, Stephen. USA Today. Rain out: China aims to control Olympics weather. 29 Feb. 2008.

"WHO | Air Quality and Health." *World Health Organization*. Aug. 2008. Web. 19 Feb. 2011. <http://www.who.int/mediacentre/factsheets/fs313/en/>.

"WHO | Air Quality Guidelines - Global Update 2005." *World Health Organization*. 2011. Web. 19 Feb. 2011.

<http://www.who.int/phe/health_topics/outdoorair_aqg/en/index.html#>.

Wolf, Aaron, and Joshua Newton. "Case Study Transboundary Dispute Resolution: the La Plata Basin." *Case Studies: Water Conflict Management and Transformation at OSU*. Oregon State University, 2007. Web. 19 Feb. 2011. <http://www.transboundarywaters.orst.edu/research/case_studies/La_Plata_New.htm>.

I took a lovely cruise around Chile and Argentina prior to commencing my Chile Global Intensive program with New York University in Santiago (January 2011). Here below from my video channel – YouTube.com/GreatAwakening - are 2 fun videos:

Travel Videos Chile Mountains, Glaciers, Cape Horn
http://www.youtube.com/watch?v=2dBPzsu9v9w

Travel Videos Argentina Penguins, Penguinos Argentina
http://www.youtube.com/watch?v=7tQyaO-w338

My travels throughout Chile to places like the poet Pablo Neruda's home, the place where political dissidents were murdered by the Pinochet regime, and visits to the Presidential district with Professor Patricio Navia were very memorable and enjoyable.

My fellow classmates from New York University
within the Global Affairs program in Chile
with Professor Patricio Navia.

Paul F Davis is a Geostrategist, Foreign Policy Adviser, Global Health Coach, Wellness Trainer, Disease Prevention Speaker and Food Consultant who has touched 70 Nations empowering countries to protect environmental health and people to naturally heal their bodies and achieve personal wellness body-mind-spirit. The author of several books Paul studied Global Affairs at NYU, Global Food Law at MSU and Nutrition for Disease Prevention with USF. Paul consults and speaks for Governments, Companies, the U.S. Military, Universities, and the Food and Tourism industries.

Contact (info@PaulFDavis.com) for health and wellness seminars to cure and prevent diseases and strengthen your national economy. Paul provides health coaching, global business consulting and inspirational life-changing speeches to audiences of all ages.

Social Media

PaulFDavis.com

More Books at PaulFDavis.com/booksvideos.htm

Linkedin.com/in/worldproperties

Twitter.com/PaulFDavis

Facebook.com/speakers4inspiration

Beach-Homes.org

Future Books

As the author of "The Future of Food" (volumes 1 and 2) Paul is interested in traveling throughout countries and examining their food and environmental health systems to consult and write future books to teach the world. Contact Paul if your nation and region is interested in sponsoring Paul to promote ecotourism, environmental and public health and disease prevention to reduce the economic burden of medical care and increase sustainable development.

Contact (info@PaulFDavis.com) if you would like Paul to visit, review, write and produce a video about the agriculture, food, environment and health systems in your country. Any future book ideas, topics and questions you desire Paul to address are also welcomed.

www.ingramcontent.com/pod-product-compliance
Lightning Source LLC
Chambersburg PA
CBHW070801290526
45795CB00002B/594

* 9 7 8 1 4 9 2 3 1 8 0 2 6 *